To

_____

From

_____

Date

_____

DESTROYING SATANIC WEAPONS

ISAIAH OLUJINMI

Destroying Satanic Weapons

Copyright © 2018 by Isaiah Olujinmi

Paperback ISBN: 978-1-944652-78-4

Printed in the United States of America. All rights reserved solely by the publisher. This book or parts thereof may not be reproduced in any form, stored in a retrieval system, or transmitted in any form by any means - electronic, mechanical, photocopy. Unless otherwise noted, Bible quotations are taken from the Holy Bible, King James Version. Copyright 1982 by Thomas Nelson, Inc., publishers. Used by permission.

Published by:
Cornerstone Publishing
A Division of Cornerstone Creativity Group LLC
Info@thecornerstonepublishers.com
www.thecornerstonepublishers.com
516.547.4999

Author's Contact

For booking to speak at your next event or to order bulk copies of this book please use information below:

   Phone: +1 647 362 2888
   Email: prophet2world@gmail.com

DEDICATION

This book is dedicated to the Almighty God for His divine revelation in exposing and destroying the works of darkness.

ACKNOWLEDGMENTS

To my wife, **Dr. Tosin Dotun-Olujinmi** for being an inspiration and for her relentless support with the success of this book. Rose Bosooke Olarenwaju and Hermilyn Noel for their contribution in making this book a reality.

CONTENTS

Dedication..5

Acknowledgments......................................6

Introduction...9

Chapter 1
Understanding Spiritual Warfare..................13

Chapter 2
Take Off the Evil Garments.......................17

Chapter 3
Destroying Enchantment............................33

Chapter 4
Destroying Cobweb Attack.........................41

Chapter 5
Destroying Evil Pots..................................49

Chapter 6
Destroy Evil Hands...................................57

Chapter 7
Stones of Wickedness..................................67

Chapter 8
Removing Evil Mark..................................79

About The Author..93

INTRODUCTION

Isaiah 54:17

Isaiah 54 verse 17 states that *"No weapon that is formed against thee shall prosper; and every tongue that shall rise against thee in judgment thou shalt condemn. This is the heritage of the servants of the LORD, and their righteousness is of me, saith the LORD."*

The enemy has strategic ways of attacking people especially believers of Jesus Christ. One of those ways is dispatching his many arsenal to destroy and to eventually kill. In John 10:10, the bible makes us to understand that "the thief cometh not, but for to steal, and to kill, and to destroy, I (Jesus Christ) am come that they might have life, and that they might have it more abundantly."

Many have been victims of these demonic weapons because they lack understanding of

Destroying Satanic Weapons

spiritual operations. Many also use physical strength and analytical mind to fight spiritual battle. 2 Corinthians 10: 4 states that *"For the weapons of our warfare are not carnal, but mighty through God to the pulling down of strongholds"* what the scripture simply means is that you need the power of God to challenge every satanic attack in your life. I remember the story of a brother that called me many years ago from Germany. He is of African descent and his wife is German. Every time he sleeps, he had dreams of people flogging him and when he wakes up his entire body will be full of marks and with excruciating pain. So, when he called me, I prayed with him and gave him divine instructions which he followed and the Lord gave him victory. Yet the powers flogging him were not done, The attackers now started dealing with his wife. Each time she wakes up in the morning, she sees her skin reaping apart due to flogging in her sleep. The pain was unbearable but with intense faith-filled fervent prayers the Lord intervened, and the family has been rejoicing ever since.

The devil is fearless when it comes to using his wicked weapons and he will stop at nothing to destroy lives that have a colourful destiny.

Hence, the reason why some of his weapons will be exposed in this book so you can fight a good fight of faith.

Chapter 1

UNDERSTANDING SPIRITUAL WARFARE

Life is a battle and everyone on the earth faces one battle or the other which is why Job 14:1 says Man that is born of a woman is of few days and full of trouble. This shows that many are fighting the battle of life in various areas of life, Even God was described in Exodus 15:3 as the man of War, we are also expected as his soldiers on earth to engage in spiritual warfare. Spiritual warfare is an act of fighting satanic powers assigned to hinder your life and destiny. Spiritual warfare is battling powers assigned to steal, to kill and destroy your life.

Ephesians 6:12 'For we wrestle not against flesh and blood, but against principalities, against powers, against

Destroying Satanic Weapons

rulers of darkness of this world, against spiritual wickedness in high places."

There are few important things to bring out of this passage

1. To wrestle is to fight against an opponent. To struggle with a difficulty or a problem. To wrestle is to have brutal confrontation, To have constant and continual fight.

2. Our battle is not with any human, as a soldier the rule of engagement is not with civilians but with opposing soldiers.

3. We have Four categories of powers that we have to confront: (a) Principalities: is the entity ruling over an environment, territory of jurisdiction. (b) Powers: Demons set over territories to carry out orders from satan. (c) Rulers of darkness of this world: This are world rulers that emphasizes the enemies intention to control. (d) Spiritual wickedness in high places: Powers that plot hardship and difficulty from heavenly realm.

Spiritual Warfare started in heaven according to *Revelation 12:7 "And there was war in heaven Michael and his angels fought against the dragon, and the dragon fought and his angels."*

The devil's defeat brought about battles for man "Woe to the inhabitants of the earth and of the sea, for the devil is come down with great wrath because he knoweth that he hath but a short time. (Revelation 12:12b). Everything that occurs in the physical world is directly connected to the battle being waged in the spiritual world which is why we must learn, understand and be active in strategic warfare so that we will not be snared by the enemy. The battle of life is real and serious. Many are in battle right now, some have lost all they had, some are already a casualty of war and many have lost lives and families through this battles but understand that God is with you and he will strengthen you and you begin to fight for your life.

Psalms 144:1 'Blessed be the LORD my strength which teach my hands to war and my fingers to fight'.

WHY MUST YOU FIGHT?

1. You must fight because you have been occupying the wrong position for to long.
2. You must fight to recover all the enemy

has stolen from you.

3. You fight to safeguard your life and your destiny.

4. You must fight because the devil only understands violence.

5. Battles has already been declared against you whether you know it or not.

6. You must fight because sometimes to gain peace war must be enacted.

7. You must fight so that stubborn situation will be eliminated.

8. You must fight to deliver yourself from bondage and oppression.

9. You must fight because opposition positions you for your promotions.

10. You must fight to enjoy your prophetic destiny.

Chapter 2

TAKE OFF THE EVIL GARMENTS

Zechariah 3:1-5

The standard of God on garments has not changed. Joseph's coat of many colours foretold his glorious and fruitful destiny (Genesis 37:3). Likewise his prison garments was later changed to a princely garment (Genesis 41:14). We also see how blind Bartimaeus beggarly garment was taken off him so as to receive recovering of sight and total restoration. (Mark 10:46-52). In Genesis 3:21, Adam and Eve made leaves to cover themselves from shame and sin which was not adequate for their covering then God now gave them the appropriate garment (animal skin) to cover them and to make atonement for their sins.because without the blood there

Destroying Satanic Weapons

can be no atonement of sins. Adam and Eve thought they needed a physical garment to cover their nakedness but God made them realise that their spiritual covering was more important. A spiritual garment is what covers the individual in the realm of the spirit. What garment are you wearing? According to the bible, good garments are described in Colossians 3:12, put on therefore, as elect of God, holy and beloved, bowels of mercy, kindness, humility, gentleness, and patience. Another good spiritual clothing was mentioned in Isaiah 61:3, God gives us "the garment of praise for the garment of heaviness". We are also to put on the whole armour of God as mentioned in Ephesians 6:10. Another good spiritual garment is to put on the Lord Jesus Christ (Romans 13:14) so that the character of Christ can be reflected in our walk and lives.

Evil garments on the other hand are prepared in the demonic kingdom to bring chaos, calamity, and destruction into people's lives. The garment you are wearing in the spiritual realm can affect your physical life. For example, Joshua the high priest was confronted by Satan because of the filthy garments he was wearing of si (Zechariah 3:1-4). Other evil garments include garments of affliction, rejection, condemnation, sorrow, stagnation, and misfortune. It is possible for to wear the right garment at the wrong place and time for instance, a three- piece suit is a decent garment but it is inappropriate to be worn to work on a construction site as a construction worker, nevertheless, this same garment will be an acceptable and appropriate attire to be worn to the board meeting of a construction company. Matthew 22: 11-14, tells of a man that showed up at a wedding without the proper garment and he was bound hand and foot and casted out into the outer darkness. Close your eyes and pray like this:

- Every wrong garment I am wearing that is causing bad luck in my life, let it catch fire in Jesus name.

- Evil garments that I am wearing that is prolonging problems in my life, be destroyed in Jesus name.

EVIL GARMENTS

Evil garments can be defined as demonic items of clothing that could affect your physical manifestation. Evil garments can be visible or invisible. For example, an individual can dress up in a visible demonic attire to carry out satanic rituals. Example of such are traditional garments worn by idol worshippers in parts of Africa, Asia, the Caribbean and South America. Also, in some parts of the Western world, there are attires that are worn to represent satanic worship for instance, the scary evil garments worn during the Halloween by the Druids in Europe and North America. There are also invisible filthy garments as illustrated in Zechariah 3:1-4. Joshua the high priest wore filthy garments which might be unseen to the visible eyes but serve as an evil spiritual covering.

CHARACTERISTIC OF EVIL GARMENTS

- Evil garments are garments that introduce affliction and destruction into people's life.

- Evil garments are a tool the devil uses to keep its victims in bondage.

- Evil garments can terminate destiny;

- Evil garments can be used to enforce

demonic stronghold in a person's life;

- Evil garments can cause an individual to lose his/her rightful position;

- Evil garments can cause spiritual and physical death;

- Evil garments can cause ridicule, shame and disgrace;

- Evil garments can exposes an individual to demonic attacks and physical rejection;

- Evil garments can make you a victim of failure and stagnancy;

- Evil garments can make you have destructive dreams such as seeing yourself wearing rags or being naked;

- Evil garments can distance your helpers from you.

- Evil garments can deflect blessings from you.

- Evil garments can hinder favour and cause unusual hatred.

- Evil garments can release the spirit of heaviness, fear and worry.

- Evil garments can destroy your real identity.
- Evil garment can cause poverty.

TYPES OF GARMENT

The type of garment you wear determines what you attract or what is attracted to you. We see in the book of Genesis 3:21 that Adam and Eve were clothed with shame and they made garments of leaves to cover themselves. But God showed up and gave them a proper garment and skin to atone for their sins and cover them. Many are in similar situations today attempting to use physical solutions to solve spiritual problems. 2 Corinthians 10:14. Therefore, evil garments must be seriously dealt with.

Filthy Garment: This type of garment was the one Joshua the high priest was wearing (Zechariah 3:1-5). It causes satanic contention. It gives the enemy an upper hand over one's life and it hinders the flow of heavenly blessings. An individual that has a filthy garment is likely to experience rejection and hatred.

Garment of Shame: This was what symbolically the adulterous woman was wearing in John 8:3-9. The garment of shame will usually manifests as either complete or partial nakedness in the dream. . Garment of shame causes humiliation. It also causes false accusation as well as demonic delays. Garment of shame can also make you withdraw from your place of help causing you to walk into the snares laid down by the enemy.

Garment of Affliction: *Isaiah 54:11 "O thou afflicted tossed with tempst and not comforted, behold I will lay thy stones with fair colours and lay thy foundation with sapphires".* Garment of affliction causes pain and despair. It injects suffering, sorrow and difficulty into one's life. It can also causes mental and physical distress.

Garment of Infirmity: this is a very dangerous garment which attracts diseases and sickness into the life of an individual. Some of this sicknesses and diseases defy medical treatments and natural approaches. Luke 8:43 tells us of a woman with the issue of blood that had the garment of infirmity. *"And a woman having an issue of blood twelve years which and spent all her living upon physicians, neither could be healed of any".* We can conclude that the agenda of the garment of infirmity is to destroy the individual and ruin their finances.

Garment of Poverty: Proverbs 24: 33-34. These garment makes you borrow to eat instead of lending to nations. It makes you have a beggarly attitude towards life. Struggle becomes a lifestyle whilst others are enjoying the best things life can bring. You may even have money but can't give an account of you spent it, the garment of poverty causes wastage. A person afflicted by the garment of poverty will experience some of the following.

- Begging to buy basic things like food.
- Difficulty in all areas employment.
- Dreams of walking bare footed.
- Dreams of wearing rags.
- Dreams of losing bags, purses or wallets.
- Being ignored by potential spouses or helpers of destiny
- Lack of favor
- Unusual hatred and rejection
- There is a transfer of blessing

Grave Clothes: These garments operate

physically and spiritually like the one on Lazarus. They were used to bind him hands and legs. John 11:43-44. When the spirit behind the grave clothes is in operation in the life of a person, he/she will experience the following:

- Periodic sickness, sometimes unexplainable.
- Seeing dead relatives or people in dreams.
- Seeing oneself dead in the dreams or funeral being conducted for one.
- Suicidal thoughts.
- Perceived Aroma or smell of death.
- Financial attacks.
- Eating, talking and partying with dead people.
- Seeing oneself at the graveyard.
- Marital, career and business struggles and hardship.
- People calling your name strangely without you seeing them.

Garment of Leprosy: Leviticus 13:47 Leprosy is an infectious disease that causes severe, disfiguring skin sores and nerve damage in the arms, legs, and skin area around the body. The disease is often surrounded by negative stigma that causes the individual to be an outcast in the society.Leprosy is a feared disease and people that has it are often isolated because many think it's curse placed on the individuals. Family and friends abandons them,they are evicted out of their homes, fired from their workplace and completely neglected by Society. When an individual is wearing the garment of leprosy they begin to lose spiritual sensitivity and the enemy begins to increase its attack on the individual by isolating them from the ones that will help them; finances becomes affected because the hands has been disfigured by the effect t of this garment , movement and progress are restricted due to the attack on the leg and the entire life continues to deteriorate by constant attacks and pain. These garments are damaging and cause severe disfiguring impact on people physically and spiritually. Agenda of the garment is to:

- Gradually incapacitate you.

- To reduce your growth and increase.

- Physical and Spiritual isolation.

- Rejection. Anywhere you go, rejection becomes a norm. People avoid you.

- To cause internal and emotional damage.

- Disfigure your body shape.

- Open you up to satanic attacks.

Transfer Garment: Genesis 26:14: *"And Rebekah took godly raiment of her oldest son Esau, which was with her in the house and put them upon Jacob her younger son"*. Anytime your garment is stolen or transferred people begin to enjoy the blessing due to you and you will begin to experience the individual's sufferings.

Many lives have been caged and destroyed because of these acts of wickedness. Some of you are suffering today because your garment is being worn by someone else. I pray for you today, anyone wearing your garment in order to divert or convert your blessing be stripped naked in Jesus' name.

Garment of Enslavement: This is a giant of profitless hard work. The children of Israel wore the garment in Egypt. They worked while Pharaoh enjoyed the fruits of their labour. You know you should be the master, but you are continually a servant. People are using your star and virtue to prosper and to shine while you suffer and struggle. Pray this prayer with holy anger: Any power using my virtue and star to prosper leaving me poor, your time is up, return my virtue, return my star now by fire in Jesus name.

Garment of Insanity: This is a serious and destructive garment as witnessed in Mark 5: the man with the unclean spirit that dwells in the graveyard. When the spirit of insanity is in display it can destroy people and cause insanity. The garment makes you to lose focus, attacks your memory so you become forgetful, sometimes causes dangerous headaches. Pray this prayer: Every garment of insanity placed upon my life catch fire now in Jesus' name.

The characteristics of the spirit of insanity are:

- Hallucinating, seeing, hearing and feeling unseen things,
- Seeing or dreaming about mad people.
- Attack against your mind.
- Sleeplessness, being unable to sleep soundly.

- Strange things moving in your body and head.
- Hatred.

HOW TO TAKE OFF EVIL GARMENTS

- Change your lifestyle by repenting from your old ways.
- Make confession of any sin known and unknown that has led to you putting on an evil garment.
- Ask the Lord to replace any evil garment in your life with a new one.
- Pray that any evil garment in your life begin to roast by fire.
- Enter your season of rest.

PRAYER TO TAKE OFF EVIL GARMENT

1. Every filthy garment on my life, catch fire now in Jesus name.
2. Grave cloth upon my destiny, I am not your candidate roast by fire in Jesus name.

Destroying Satanic Weapons

3. Every power assigned to steal or exchange my coat of many colours for a satanic garment, die in Jesus name,

4. By the blood of Jesus, any inherited garment of poverty on my life, burn to ashes in Jesus name.

5. Garment of affliction, catch fire now in Jesus name,

6. By the power of the holy ghost, I put on my royal garment in Jesus name.

7. Every garment in my life magnetizing problem to me, catch fire now, in Jesus name.

8. Garment of shame and disgrace, I take you off my life in Jesus name.

9. My Father in heaven let the garment of untimely death be removed from my life in ancestral garment of bondage upon me catch fire and roast to ashes in Jesus name.

10. Blood of Jesus neutralize the effect of every evil garment on my life.

11. Lord put me the garment of favour, honor and greatness in Jesus name.

12. Every good thing that was exchanged in my life, be restored in Jesus name.

13. Angel of the Lord put upon me now the garment of prosperity in Jesus name.

14. By the power in the blood of Jesus, I enter into a new season.

Chapter 3

DESTROYING ENCHANTMENT

Numbers 23:23
"Surely there is no enchantment against Jacob, neither is there any divination against Israel, according to this time it shall be said of Jacob and of Israel what hath God wrought?"

Enchantment is a demonic device or weapon used by the enemy to cast spells on people. It also consists of jinxes and hexes, occultism and practice of magic, voodoo and bewitchment. Enchantment is usually empowered by blood sacrifice and evil covenant, that in turn affects or destroys businesses, careers, ministries, marriages, and individual lives.

We see in the Scriptures that Balaam was hired as an enchanter to place a curse upon

Destroying Satanic Weapons

the Nation of Israel (Numbers 22:6). May the Lord disgrace Anyone hired to place a curse upon your life, in Jesus' name. So many lives have been destroyed and incapacitated because of this demonic device called enchantment, I remember the case of a young lady that called me a couple of years ago saying a voice woke her up on a Saturday morning to go to work. Usually she works Monday through Friday because she works in corporate America (businesses of this sort do not open on weekends). However, she ignored the voice, but the voice became stronger and finally, she obeyed and went to her office. Fortunately, the security guard let her in and as she went into her office, she found two of her co-workers burning candles and incense, and chanting all over the office. They were surprised to see her, and when she confronted them, They quickly stopped what they were doing and left. God used this lady to avert what could have been a demonic manipulation in her place of work. I pray for you that no enchantment shall have any effect over your life and destiny in Jesus' name

There are different forms of enchantments and understanding them will better equip you

Bewitchment: is an act of using sorcery to capture and control the life of an individual.

"But there was a certain man called Simon which before time in the same city used sorcery, and bewitched the people of Samaria, giving out that himself was some great one" (Acts 8:9).

With the weapon of sorcery in the hand of this wicked man, a whole city of people was bewitched.

After prayers one evening, two of my spiritual children went shopping and they saw a woman screaming and shouting near the shops. They managed to talk to her and discovered that she had been to a palm reader next door, and as soon she left the palm reader, she began to lose her mind and was taken to the hospital. They discharged her from the hospital and took her to the palm-reader to inquire what he did to her, the palm-reader touched her head and sent her away. My spiritual daughters found her in the state of confusion and delusion; they prayed with her and she was set free.

Bewitchment is a satanic weapon that perverts the truth. It makes people work and operate under satanic blindness. Bewitchment causes demonic possession and oppression of its victims. Bewitchment is enforced by the use spells, charms and incantations to cage and keep people in bondage. Bewitchment is a weapon of great manipulation. This is why the bible says in Galatians 3:1 *"O foolish Galatians, who hath bewitched you, that ye should not obey the truth, before whose eyes Jesus Christ hath been evidently set forth, crucified among you?"*

Charms: are dangerous part of enchantment used in destroying lives. According to Deuteronomy 18:10-11, a charmer should not be found among you. A lady ran to me for deliverance in my early years of ministry in 2001. She had been abused by the man she was in a relationship with. Prior to that, she had used a love portion to bewitch the man but as soon as the spell was broken the man became abusive towards her. Say this prayer, Every charm used to hold me bound, be broken now in Jesus' name.

Charm infused waist beads, demonic amulets, portions and much more are used to hypnotize, manipulate destinies and keep their victims bound. May you not be ensnared by evil charms and amulets in Jesus' name.

SYMPTOMS OF AN ENCHANTMENT VICTIM

- The victim will be operating under the effects of a curse.

- Stagnancy will be experienced.

- When you are under the effect of an enchantment, you will be having strange dreams of being pursued to by a murderer, dreams of being sentenced to death or prison, dreams of attack from deadly animals.

- Manipulation to do the wrong things and make wrong decisions.

- Strange attacks over your life especially at midnight.

- Having a feeling of eerie presence in your home or environment.

- Hearing strange voices that tells you to kill yourself or do some other strange things.

- Financial struggles

- Career and business inadequacy.

- Vicious cycles of pain and fruitlessness

- Unexplainable sicknesses.
- Periodic and seasonal attacks over your life.
- Accidents and tragedies.
- Difficulty in praying and reading the word.
- Misfortune and lack of favor.
- Mental instability and memory loss.
- Marital problems, always fighting and not knowing the cause.
- When the things of God become irrelevant to you.
- Insomnia
- Feeling of being monitored.
- There are unexplainable things happening around you.

HOW TO DESTROY ENCHANTMENT

- Give your life totally to God by repenting from your sins.
- Pray that the blood of Jesus begins to speak for you (Hebrew 12:24).

- Cancel all demonic enchantment.
- Command the elements (sun, moon and stars) not to cooperate with your enchanters.
- Command everything spoken into the atmosphere or programmed into the earth against you to be cancelled.
- Command the powers behind the enchanters to be destroyed in Jesus name.
- Command everything you have lost through enchantments to be recovered and restored in Jesus name.

PRAYER TO DESTROY ENCHANTMENT

1. My Father, my God, let your power descend mightily upon me in Jesus name.
2. I break the yoke of enchantment against my life in Jesus name.
3. Every enchantment and divination pronounced against my destiny back fire in Jesus name.
4. Every demonic decree programmed into the day and night against me, be destroyed by the blood of Jesus.

Destroying Satanic Weapons

5. Any power calling my name in the middle of the night, receive the thunder of God in Jesus name.

6. Every demonic fasting and praying against me, roast by fire in Jesus name,

7. Any form of evil sacrifice made to cage my life, lose your power and be destroyed in Jesus name.

8. Any demonic pot of enchantment cooking my glory and star, be broken now in Jesus name.

9. Broom of enchantment sweeping away my blessings, be destroyed by fire in Jesus name.

10. Every wicked gathering summoning my spirit and soul at midnight, be scattered by fire in Jesus name.

11. Charms and spells done to destroy my life, be consumed by fire in Jesus name.

12. Any enchantment troubling my life, be exposed and be disgraced in Jesus name.

13. My glory, my star be restored in Jesus name.

Chapter 4

DESTROYING COBWEB ATTACK

Isaiah 54:17

Cobweb attacks is one of the demonic weapons that witches and marine powers uses to empty and destroy the lives of people. The viscous attacks usually occur or starts in the dream and then manifest itself in the physical. People under the relentless attack of cobwebs feel it in their bodies. Some in particular areas like the face and the head. They may also takeover your properties; such as cars, houses and clothing. You may not be their only victim. They can also project the attack to your children and everyone around you.

Demonic cobweb is an anti-breakthrough

weapon projected to stop you from experiencing your destined change in life. It often manifests during or before a life transforming breakthrough such as marriage, starting a new business, about to win a court case, being granted documentation, expecting a promotion or even during pregnancy.

The ultimate agenda of the demonic cobweb is to stop your advancement. As a believer, it is very important to understand God has the ultimate power and has apportioned it to us. Behold I give you power to tread upon serpent and scorpion and all the power of the enemy and nothing shall by any means hurt you. (Luke 10:19)

PURPOSE OF DEMONIC COBWEB

- They manipulate and/or influence you to make wrong choices especially in marriage, and lead you to wrong places to seek for help;

- They make you miss the timing of God for your life by taking you away from where you are supposed to be blessed. *"Those that be planted in the house of the Lord shall flourish in the courts of our God" (Psalms 92:13).*

- This power displaces you from where you are supposed to be planted to succeed.

- They make everything you do to become unproductive.

- Those under demonic cobweb attacks experience death - death of businesses, marriages, relationships, health etc. they work hard with little or nothing to show for their hard work; always dead. The reason is because everything in their life seems inactive. The individual may experience dead business, may be educated but have nothing to show for it.

- They act to cause a detour in your life or to misdirect your path;

- They are assigned to render you useless;

- They derail your destiny;

- Demonic cobweb act as an embargo to hinder your progress.

MANIFESTATIONS OF DEMONIC COBWEBS MANIPULATION

- Frequent setbacks
- Demonic delays
- Release of evil judgment
- Demonic accusation
- Evil counsel
- Poverty
- Confusion and diversion
- Isolation
- They imprison the victim
- Discouragement

When symptoms are manifested physically, you are to fight for your life. According Isaiah 54:17 no weapons formed against you shall prosper. So, when you notice these manifestations, it's time to fight.

Demonic Cobweb

This can manifest as:

- Struggle.

- Helpers avoiding you.
- Delay to breakthrough.
- Failure at the edge to breakthrough.
- Stagnation.
- Blockages no way out of certain situation.
- Miscarriage of pregnancy, visions and ideas.
- Rejection.
- Unnecessary hatred against you.
- Discomfort.
- Barrenness and unfruitfulness.
- Periodic sickness.
- Seasonal attacks.
- Attack in the dreams.
- Prayerlessness.

STEPS TO DELIVERANCE

1. Receive Jesus as your personal Savior.

Prayer of repentance and salvation:

Lord Jesus I have sinned against you, have

Destroying Satanic Weapons

mercy upon me, cleanse me of all my sins and iniquity. Wash me with your blood so I can be whiter than snow; I believe you died for me and rose on the 3rd day. I believe in my heart and confess with my mouth that you are Lord. Thank you for accepting me.

2. Avoid sin; flee every appearance of evil.

3. Ask God to open your spiritual eyes to see the signs.

4. Reverse evil projective and declaration against you.

5. Pray against witchcraft weapon used against you.

6. Arrest the powers behind the cobweb.

7. Release fire of the Holy Spirit against the particular area of attack.

8. Kill the spiders.

9. Cover yourself in the blood of Jesus and release fire against cobwebs attack.

PRAYER

1. Every demonic cobweb programed by witches and wizards into my life catch fire in Jesus' name.

2. Covenanted cobwebs operating from by bloodline be roasted by fire, in Jesus name.

3. Altar of witchcraft cobweb in my household be smashed to pieces in Jesus name.

4. Satanic cobweb blocking my breakthrough be roasted by fire in Jesus name.

5. My father, my Lord arise in your power and release me from the stronghold of demonic cobweb in Jesus name.

6. Every demonic spider assigned to frustrate my life, die in Jesus name.

7. You witchcraft spider flying contrary to my destiny fell down and die in Jesus name.

8. Demonic agent of cobweb around my life be expose and die in Jesus name.

9. Any person that is hindering my prayers through demonic cobweb be disgraced in Jesus name.

10. Every wicked power of cobweb enforcing stubborn problems in my life die by fire in Jesus name.

Destroying Satanic Weapons

11. Cobwebs in my head, hands, face, feet, mouth, leg, back and body roast by fire in Jesus name.

12. Every damage done to my life by demonic cobwebs be repaired in Jesus name.

13. All my diverted blessings by demonic cobweb is restored back to me in Jesus name.

14. I break myself loose from the hold of demonic cobweb in Jesus name.

15. I break free from the curses and covenant of demonic cobweb.

Chapter 5

DESTROYING EVIL POTS

Ezekiel 11:1-1, Micah 3:1

CAULDRONS

Cauldrons are pots made out of clay - evil cauldrons (pot) are witchcraft weapons use to cause mayhem in the life of a victim. They can be owned by individuals, families or cities. They can also be transferred from generation to generation. Sometimes in families where these pots are operating, personal items like hair, clothing, fingernail, placenta, blood, shoes, and picture are placed in the cauldrons.

In this case people's lives can be programmed with the pot. Evil pots (cauldrons) can be seen in places and cultures around the world;

like Africa, Asia, Haiti, America, Caribbean and even in the Western region of the world (America, Europe, Australia). They are used and operated by psychics and fortune tellers.

The victims' lives are programmed to these pots so that they can be manipulated and controlled (Micah 3:1-3). Communities and even an entire nation can be under these wickedness weapons of witchcraft (Ezekiel 11:31-7).

- They are used for manipulating lives; causing a detour and diversion from God's original purpose.

- They are used for incantation: The victims' names are and images are called out from the pot to kill and cause harm.

- Evil cauldrons are used for bewitchment or control; in others words one can be controlled or bewitched from any pot of the world.

- When lives and destinies are cooked in the evil pots, the victims begin to experience unusual sickness, the victim's career is also attacked with the aim of destroying the person completely.

- They are used for enchantments. Leviticus 19:26 states that *"Ye shall not eat anything with the blood neither shall he use enchantment nor observe times"*.

- Arrows can be fired from an evil pot to cause affliction in the life of their victims. Psalm 11:2 *"For behold the wicked bend their bow they make ready their arrow upon the string to shot in darkness at the upright in heart"*. Arrows are fired to cause miscarriage of pregnancies, high blood pressure, mental attacks and abnormalities in a new-born life.

- Evil pots are used to summon individuals for satanic judgment. I remember praying for a man in Germany who was married to German woman; he would experience being flogged in the dream and will wake up with marks in his body along with excruciating pain. After intense prayers, the attack shifted from the man to his wife but through deliverance prayer, victory was granted to them.

Prayer: Every evil voice calling my name with an evil pot to punish me, be choked by fire in Jesus' name.

Destroying Satanic Weapons

- Evil pots are used to eat victims' organs: Eaters of flesh and drinkers of blood cook and eat up the organs of their victims in a pot. They cook their vital organs like the heart, the lungs, intestines, the liver and the kidney. Victims are sometimes through dream manipulation, forced to participate in the eating of their own organs. I pray that the fire of the Holy Ghost will come upon you now, and I decree Isaiah 49: 26 upon your enemies- that God will feed them that oppress you with their own flesh and they shall be drunken with their own blood as with sweet wine in Jesus' name.

Prayer: You eaters of flesh and drinkers of blood assigned against, me begin to eat your own flesh and drink your own blood by fire in Jesus' name.

- They are used to cause mischief and give wicked counsel to derail their victims at the edge of their breakthrough (Ezekiel 11:2).

Prayer: Anyone using evil cauldron to program mischief into my life, your time is up, I prophecy against you, receive the judgment of God in Jesus' name.

- Evil pots are used to cause mayhem and havoc. Evil is programmed into people's life through the evil pot to bring sickness, confusion, limited progress, accidents, tragedy and sadness.

Prayer: Witchcraft pot causing evil in my life be broken in the Name of Jesus.

THE POWERS BENEATH EVIL POTS

Now there are several powers and behind these wicked operations:

- **Witchcraft Powers:** They are assigned to eat flesh and drink blood.
- **Household Wickedness:** They craft wickedness against you from within the family to destroy you.
- **Killers of Destiny:** These ones monitor your destiny from childhood and eventually set a trap made for the destiny of the individual to be destroyed eventually terminated.
- **Evil Priest:** They chant incantations from evil altars to attack their victims. They also use divination through evil pot.
- Territorial environmental powers.

MANIFESTATION OF ATTACK BY EVIL CAULDRON

- Undetectable.
- Sickness.
- Satanic delay.
- Anti-breakthrough power.
- Demonic dreams and stature attacks.
- Untimely Premature death.
- Blood attack- i.e. have high blood pressure.
- Non-achievement and demotion.
- High temperature from within.
- Embargo and stagnation.
- Poverty and leaking pockets.
- Helpers far away from you.
- Anti-clockwise spirit.

SOLUTION

1. Repent from sins and deal with it aggressively.

2. Humble yourself and surrender to Jesus.

3. Let forgiveness reign supreme.

4. Take the battle to the enemy.

5. Ask God to open your eyes to know the source of your problem.

6. Issue judgment on evil pots.

7. Cover your life in the blood of Jesus.

PRAYER

1. Evil Pot programmed against my life, be smashed to ashes in Jesus name.

2. Every evil pot cooking away areas of my life your time is up: break, break, break in Jesus' name.

3. The powers behind the evil pot appear and die in Jesus' name.

4. You powers manipulating my destiny by the evil pot be destroyed in Jesus' name.

5. I released my life from evil bewitchment and control in the name of Jesus.

6. I separate myself from any image reporting

Destroying Satanic Weapons

my life inside the satanic pot in Jesus name.

7. Household witches cooperating with enchanters to cage my life become confused in Jesus' name.

8. This city (mention the city you live) will not be a cauldron in the name of Jesus

9. Every strongman using evil pots to feed on my life and goodness vomit them and die in Jesus name.

10. Everything in my life that has been destroyed by evil pot be restored in Jesus name.

11. Anyone chanting at midnight into an evil pot against me receive the thunder of God in Jesus' name.

12. Any sickness in my life programmed from an evil pot backfire now Jesus' name.

13. Let there be a restoration of all things stolen from my life by the power of darkness in Jesus' name.

14. Angels of God search through the land, the sea and the atmosphere, wherever any evil pot has been buried against me, smash them to pieces in Jesus' name.

Chapter 6

DESTROY EVIL HANDS

1 Kings 13:1- 4, Psalms 140:4

Evil hands are a dangerous weapon used by the agent of darkness to destroy destinies. Evil hands can be invisible, therefore not visible to the physical sight. They operate from the spiritual realm and can also be damaging physically. We will expose these weapons, so you can pray effectively for victory.

Evil hands are hands:

- That places limitation upon people's lives;

- That exchange an individual's destiny;

- That steal good things away from your life;

- That press you down while sleeping by

projecting into your dreams;

- That manipulates evil and destroys destiny;
- That introduce affliction and sickness into their victim's life;
- That plant evil into marriage, career, business, studies, body, church and ministries;
- That write and report destructive charges against people;
- That disable and amputate destinies;
- That Push good things away from you.

OPERATION OF EVIL HANDS

- Evil hands operate by laying of hands physically or in the dream to destroy a person's destiny. A couple of years ago, my spiritual daughters brought a woman to church that consulted a psychic, who laid hands on her and she ran mad. If not for prayer and divine intervention the enemy would have prevailed.
- Evil hands operate by cutting off people's hair while asleep and the victim wakes up

to see patches on their heads. In other words, the victim's God given glory has been tampered with (Judges 16).

- Evil hands write evil report against the victim, especially in their health, finances, marriage and business (Colossians 2:14).

- Evil hands steal birthrights as Jacob did with Esau (Genesis 27).

- Blessings are converted to curses by evil hands.

- Evil hands are always out to destroy lives and destinies.

- Evil hands exchange people's glory for another.

- Evil hands put marks of affliction, shame, hatred, attacks, sickness, death upon victims.

Prayer: Every Mark of afflictions on my life be cancelled by the blood of Jesus.

- Evil hands cause evil plantation.

Prayer: Every plantation of destruction in my life be uprooted in Jesus name.

- Evil hands are wicked hands that drag your

life down when you are trying to be lifted.

- Evil hands cause defeat and setbacks every time you are at the edge of success or breakthrough; they create problems that make it far from you.

- Evil hands build coffins and dig graves for people. They program premature or untimely death.

- Arrows and demonic stones are thrown at people via their operations these include stones of death and arrows of destruction.

- Evil hands operate by burying a person's life and every good thing that belongs to them which includes money, marriage, organs, even their own hands.

- They create an effigy that represent their victims and begin to puck away part of the effigy to attack the victim's person.

Prayer: Any image repressing my life at the hands of the wicked, I separate my life from you in Jesus' name.

- Whatever evil judgments and evil verdict against you. These manifestations vary in form such as divorce, departure letters, sack letters, and immigration deportations.

- Evil hands hinder your celebration and testimony. They make sure you don't celebrate or testify.

- Evil hands erect evil altars to gain access into your life. Altars are created to cause demonic blockages.

- Evil hands prepare evil garments. People's lives are covered with evil garments to block/hinder good things from locating them.

- Evil hands cause stagnation. It is behind rising and falling. They tie their victims to a certain spot, preventing them from moving forwarding or progressing.

Prayer: Every power causing stagnation in my life roast by fire in Jesus' name

SIGNS OF ATTACK BY EVIL HANDS

- Being pressed in your dream.
- Accident.
- Periodic sickness.

- Hostage.
- Abortion and miscarriages.
- Mental blockage and lunacy.
- Oppression and torment.
- Limitation.
- Diversion and confusion.
- Poverty and lack.
- Demonic weights and blockages.
- Not enjoying the fruit of your labor.

SATANIC POWERS BEHIND THE OPERATIONS

- **Spiritual Thieves:** Demonic spirits signed to be stealing for you.

- **Glory Exchangers:** They exchange your better glory for theirs.

- **Witchcraft Power:** They appear in your dream and to suppress you.

- **Evil Author Personalities:** These include wicked pastors, bosses or parents.

- **Marine Power:** They send their agents to monitor your life and frustrate you by blocking your blessings and miracles from manifesting.

- **Diviners and Enchanters:** These are powers that program evil into people's lives by chanting and invoking demons. They also use evil mirrors, demonic candles, crystal balls and strange weapons such as playing drums against their victims.

PRAYER

- I shall not dance to any demonic drum beat in Jesus' name.

- **Dream Attackers:** These include powers that raid you at night and attack you in your sleep.

- **Astral Power:** These are powers that project themselves and force themselves on their victims by having sexual intercourse with them thereby robbing their victims of valuable virtues.

- **Graveyard spirits and spirits of death and hell:** They come as dark shadows to touch their victims and to cause untimely death.

- **Spirit of Pharaoh:** These are satanic powers that place their prey in prolonged bondage and struggle.

- **Familiar Powers:** These powers hire prophets like Balaam to place a curse upon the their victims.

SOLUTIONS

1. Repent from known and unknown sin.
2. Forgive people that have offended you.
3. Pray and fast.
4. Pray targeted prayer.
5. Close every door opened to the enemy in your life.
6. Have faith in God and his ability to deliver you from demonic hands.
7. Prayer of Recovery and Restoration.
8. Cover yourself and family in the Blood of Jesus and surround them with the fire of the Holy Ghost.

9. Cut off demonic hands from your life. (How? Explain to the reader how this can be done)

10. Implore the hand of God to fight for you

PRAYER

1. You evil hand troubling my life, be cut off in Jesus' name.

2. Sword of God, cut off every hand of poverty from every area of my life in Jesus' name.

3. Hand of bad luck hindering my blessings, be consumed by fire in Jesus' name.

4. Evil hand of unrepentant household wickedness upon my life, wither by fire in Jesus' name

5. Every wicked hand lifted against me between the hours of 12.00am and 3am, be struck by the thunder of God in Jesus' name.

6. Every evil handwriting written against my destiny, marriage, carrier, health, children, and business, be cancelled by the blood

of Jesus'.

7. Every demonic personality hindering my progress, be consumed by fire in Jesus' name.

Chapter 7

STONES OF WICKEDNESS

2 Samuel 16:6 -13, Job 41:28

Stones are hard, solid and non-metallic material, formed of mineral matter, of which rocks consist. We also know that most buildings are constructed with stone. However, stones have been used to destroy and damage lives. Acts 7: 58 says, "And they cast him out of the city and stoned him: and the witnesses laid down their clothes at a young man's feet, whose name was Saul."

Stephen, as recorded in the Scripture, was stoned to death. Many have suffered various attacks in their lives through the stones of wickedness.

Destroying Satanic Weapons

"And that we may be delivered from unreasonable and wicked men; for all men have not faith." (2 Thessalonians 3:2).

Stones in the hands of the wicked can be a dangerous weapon. Wickedness depicts evil, which means that evil is present both physically and spiritually.

What are Stones of Wickedness?

- Stones of wickedness are stones used in destroying lives and destinies.

- Stones of wickedness are weapons of death.

- They can be planted in the body of an individual.

- They can be used as a weapon of attack in the dream.

- Stones of wickedness can be used to block promotion and resurrection. "And, behold, there was a great earthquake: for the angel of the Lord descended from heaven, and came and rolled back the stone from the door, and sat upon it." - Matthew 28:2.

- Stones of wickedness can be inherited

through the bloodline because of covenant made in the family line.

- Stones of wickedness can be a monument of demonic trafficking
- Stones of wickedness cause injury to their victim.
- An altar can be erected against an individual, group, or gathering with the stone of wickedness.
- Stones of wickedness are a demonic weapon used to keep a victim in bondage.
- Demonic sacrifices can be made on top of stones against a person.

PURPOSE OF THE STONES OF WICKEDNESS

- To kill, steal, and to destroy, (John 10:10 this is the role of the devil. Are stones of wickedness likened to Satan itself?), Acts 7:58-60.
- To cause hidden sickness.
- **Rejection:** Everywhere an individual turns, he/she encounters rejection in areas such

Destroying Satanic Weapons

as their relationships, employment, and can even face rejection from family members.

- The purpose of the stones of wickedness is that it keeps the victim in perpetual bondage. One may sometimes have dreams of being summoned in a gathering and being stoned.

- **Affliction:** non-ending problems that seem to have no solutions.

- To destroy the greatness that God has instilled in His children.

- To place a demarcation or a boundary in one's life so that they can never go beyond a certain level in their lives.

- Evil covenants and curses in the victim's bloodline will continuously be empowered.

- **Accusation:** the victim experience false accusations from friends, colleagues, and even family members (Job 8).

- Divert and waste colorful destinies.

WHO ARE THE POWERS BEHIND STONES OF WICKEDNESS?

There are several powers that use this dangerous weapon to afflict lives. Among them are:

- **Household Wickedness:** The bible states that: "a man's enemies are the members of his own household" (Micah 7:6c).

- **Destructive Powers:** They are those that stone people in their dreams.

- **Witchcraft Powers:** these include household witchcraft, mermaid witchcraft, occult witchcraft, envious and jealous people, eaters of flesh and drinkers of blood.

- **Spiritual Hired Killers:** Spirit of death and hell, which transmits internal death into the lives of the victim.

Prayer: Any spiritual hired killer on assignment to kill me, catch fire and die in the name of Jesus.

- **Demonic Judge:** These are wicked people that appear in your dream to issue demonic sentences over your life.

Destroying Satanic Weapons

- **Destiny Killers:** Those that are threatened by the progress of others and are determined to waste their destiny.

- **Evil Authority:** Includes wicked pastors, prophets, parents, and employers that want to keep their victims in bondage.

- **Demonic Presence/Powers:** These are powers that originate from the pit of hell.

- **Star Hunters:** They keep watch over their victims using demonic surveillances to abort good things in their lives.

- **Astral Powers:** Project into targeted lives or environment to torment their victims.

- **Strongmen:** The power that uses diabolical force to control a person, city, or nation.

- **Ancestral Powers**: These are powers that demand a ransom from their victims for the errors of their ancestors. They sometimes take the form of deadly animals like snakes and villains to attack their victims.

SYMPTOMS OF STONES OF WICKEDNESS

If you are experiencing any of the following symptoms, you might be a victim of Stones of Wickedness:

- Rejection.

- Sorrowful tears and pain.

Prayer: Any power assigned to cause sorrow and pain in my life, be destroyed in Jesus name.

- Confusion.

- Premature or untimely death.

- Affliction.

- Hindrances, obstacles and embargoes.

- Bondages.

- Undetectable illnesses.

- Incurable injury.

- Wastage.

- Abandonment.

- Reproach.

- Loss of peace and joy.
- Hardships and struggle.
- Limitations.
- False accusations.
- Failure at the edge of breakthrough.
- Mental attack and madness.
- Closed Doors of Opportunity.
- Lack of Progress or stagnancy.
- Repeated cycle of hardship or negative occurrences.
- Family problems; marital distress.
- Unforgiveness, or hard heartedness
- Demonic Transfer of virtues and rightful belongings.
- Shame and disgrace.

HOW TO GAIN VICTORY OVER STONES OF WICKEDNESS

1. Repentance from all known and unknown sins. Sin allows the wickedness to continue

through your dream.

2. Total surrender to Christ Jesus. Allow Christ to be the ultimate in your life; surrendering all to Him.

3. Close all open doors against the enemy and be steadfast in the Christian faith.

4. Break every evil covenant made on your behalf through your bloodline.

5. Exercise your spiritual authority by returning evil stones back to the senders.

6. Nullify all evil deposit in your by the application of the Blood of Jesus

7. Pray the prayer of resurrection for all the dead virtues in your life and for complete restoration

8. Release the Fire of God over all your surroundings and atmosphere.

9. Encircle your life with the blood of Jesus.

10. Make praise and worship your lifestyle.

Destroying Satanic Weapons

PRAYERS

1. Stone of Wickedness programmed into my life, be consumed by fire in Jesus' name.

2. Every demonic stone blocking my progress be rolled away in Jesus' name.

3. Every Goliath like enemy of my destiny, I stone you to destruction in Jesus' name.

4. Stone of Wickedness attached to my bloodline, be destroyed by fire in Jesus' name.

5. Every gathering of witches and wizards attacking through stone of wickedness, be scattered by the thunder of God in Jesus' name.

6. Blood sacrifices made upon stones to destroy my destiny, be confounded by the blood of Jesus.

7. Demonic altars erected with stones of wickedness against me, be crushed to ashes in Jesus' name.

8. Whoever is calling my name between the hours of 12 midnight to 5am into a stone, be struck by the lightening of God in Jesus' name.

9. Stones of wickedness thrown into my dream to waste my life, be destroyed by fire in Jesus' name.

10. Stones of accusation speaking against me, be silenced and return to sender in Jesus' name.

11. Whatever is representing my life at any evil altar, be removed by the angel of deliverance in Jesus' name.

12. Any stone of hindrance blocking my advancement in life, be rolled away in the name of Jesus'.

13. Evil authority that erected stones of memorial against my lifting, scatter and die in Jesus' name.

14. Every good virtue in my life that has been buried, receive the resurrection power of God in Jesus' name.

15. O Lord deliver me from the hand of the wicked in Jesus' name.

16. Every demonic angel ascending and descending over my breakthrough, be caged in Jesus' name.

Destroying Satanic Weapons

17. I cancel the effect of the stones of wickedness over my life in Jesus' name.

18. Let there be a restoration of all good things I have lost as a result of this attack in Jesus' name.

Chapter 8

REMOVING EVIL MARK

Ezekiel 9:4-6

"And the LORD said unto him, go through the midst of the city, through the midst of Jerusalem, and set a mark upon the foreheads of the men that sigh and that cry for all the abominations that be done in the midst thereof. And to the others he said in mine hearing, Go ye after him through the city, and smite: let not your eye spare, neither have ye pity: Slay utterly old and young, both maids, and little children, and women: but come not near any man upon whom is the mark; and begin at my sanctuary. Then they began at the ancient men which were before the house."

The Lord allowed marks to be placed on the foreheads of these people to punish them for their abominations, however Satan also uses evil marks to destroy the lives of its captives so that they will not be able to achieve their God given purpose in life.

WHAT IS A MARK?

- A mark is a sign or a symbol.
- A mark is a stamp.
- A mark is something that distinguishes a person from another.
- A mark is an insignia.
- A mark is a seal.
- A mark is like an emblem placed upon people.

There are physical and spiritual marks because everything that existed in the physical has its spiritual representation. Spiritual marks can either be positive or negative. When its positive you become untouchable according to Galatians 6:17: From henceforth let no man trouble me: for I bear in my body the marks of the Lord Jesus. However, when it is an evil mark, your life begins to experience all manners of satanic attacks and strange manipulation.

Prayer: My Father in heaven let people favour me because I bear on me the marks of the Lord Jesus in Jesus' name.

FACTS ABOUT EVIL MARKS

- Evil marks can be inherited through maternal or paternal bloodline.

- Evil marks exist to identify an individual in the spirit realm.

- Evil marks make favour and blessings to be far away from the bearer.

- Evil marks are usually invisible, cannot be seen with the natural eye.

- Evil marks identify you for satanic attacks and demonic manipulations.

- Evil marks are weapons used by demons to destroy lives and destinies.

- Evil marks are projected to hinder you from your prophetic destiny.

- Evil marks make your helpers not to locate you.

- Evil marks cause good things to be far away from you.

Destroying Satanic Weapons

- Evil marks are designed to make you wander in life.
- Evil marks are monitoring weapons.
- Evil marks cause suffering and stagnation.
- Evil marks place limitation and boundaries upon people.
- Evil marks are weapons of control.
- Evil marks have no regard for your age, position or societal status. In the book of Revelation 13:16-17 (KJV) John writes, "And he causeth all, both small and great, rich and poor, free and bond, to receive a mark in their right hand, or in their foreheads. And that no man might buy or sell, save he that had the mark, or the name of the beast, or the number of his name." Now there are different types of Evil Marks the devil places on people in order to demonically control them and also to continue to exert his power over them.

TYPES OF EVIL MARKS

Mark of Sorrow: A perfect example is Jabez in 1 chronicles 4:9: *"And Jabez was more honourable* *than his brethren: and his mother called his name Jabez, saying, Because I bare him with sorrow."*

Looking at this scripture, you can understand how a bad name can cause sorrow and affliction in your life. So, if you are bearing a bad name prayerfully ask the Holy Spirit to give you a new name.

PRAYER

1. O Lord, if my name is the cause of my problems, arise in your power and give me a new name in Jesus' name.

2. I cancel by the blood of Jesus sorrow and tears from my life in Jesus name.

Mark of Rejection: Everywhere you turn you face rejection and non-acceptance no matter how much you try to please people or to be at your best behaviour. People just reject you, especially in areas of importance. You are denied favours and blessing. Pray like this: I destroy every pattern of rejection operating in me in Jesus' name.

Mark of Poverty: Haggai 1:6 King James Version (KJV): *"Ye have sown much, and bring in little; ye eat, but ye have not enough; ye drink, but ye* *are not filled with drink; ye clothe you, but there is none warm; and he that earneth wages to put it into a bag with holes".* This scripture illustrates the operation of the Mark of poverty. This mark makes you to struggle in all areas of life.

Prayer: Every yoke of poverty in my life break, break, break in Jesus' name.

Mark of Death: This is when the spirit of untimely death is cycling around a person to kill or destroy the individual prematurely, so it causes periodic sickness or deadly accidents. If one is not prayerful, this mark can eventually end the life of the individual.

PRAYER

1. I shall not die prematurely in Jesus' name.
2. You vulture of untimely death cycling my life die by fire in Jesus' name.

Mark of Barrenness: *"And ye shall serve the Lord your God, and he shall bless thy bread, and thy water; and I will take sickness away from the midst of thee. There shall nothing cast their young, nor be barren, in thy land: the number of thy days I will fulfil" (Exodus 23:25-26 KJV).* Mark of barrenness leads to unfruitfulness in all areas of your life, from your marriage, career and even unproductivity in business and all other works of life. By the grace of God, we have seen in our ministry for example women that the doctors said can't give birth, giving birth to children.

Prayer: The Mark of barrenness is destroyed in my life in Jesus' Name.

Mark of Stagnation: This is a mark that keeps you in one spot without movement or progress. Many people experience this mark in their life but don't have a solution for it unless God divinely intervenes like the case of Sister Rebecca who had been looking for a job for a long time after completing her studies. On our prayer line a prophetic word came that spoke exactly to her situation the very next day she was called for an interview to resume immediately. Deuteronomy 1:6: *"The LORD our God spoke unto us in Horeb, saying, Ye have dwelt long enough in this mount"*. I prophesy into your life today that stagnation is removed from your destiny forever in Jesus' name.

Mark of Failure: When a person is operating under this mark, nothing good happens to them

Destroying Satanic Weapons

especially at the edge of their breakthrough. They begin to experience disappointment and frustration in all they do. Success that seems so near will become far. Failure becomes a lifestyle, failure in marriage, academics, business, career and in life generally. Some of these misfortunes are spiritually programmed so that a person will not accomplish God's plan for their life. I remember a young man came to me telling me how he had failed his Bar (Law) exam severally. The exam has limited attempts, so on his last attempt, he came to ask for prayers. After praying, the Spirit of God revealed the source of his problem, then I gave him instructions on what to do. To the glory of God, he passed his exam. Hallelujah! We need to understand that a lot of problems we face today have a spiritual source. I pray that God will open your eyes to know the source of your problems.

PRAYERS

1. Powers causing me to fail at the edge of my breakthrough be destroyed by fire in Jesus' mighty name.

2. Mark of failure in my life, be cancelled by the blood of Jesus in Jesus' name.

3. My Father in heaven restore to me tenfold of all the good things I have lost as a result of this evil mark in Jesus' name.

SYMPTOMS OF EVIL MARK

- When an evil mark is in operation, breakthrough and blessings become difficult to obtain.

- You experience rejection and sudden hatred everywhere you go.

- Evil Mark makes it difficult for you to be settled and established in life.

- Your helpers begin to avoid you and they also come under demonic attack in order not to help you.

- Experiencing failure at the edge of your breakthrough.

- When evil mark is in place you will begin to experience misfortune and setbacks.

- When evil mark is in operation you will begin to have bad dreams or strange attacks in your dreams.

Destroying Satanic Weapons

- Evil mark causes you to have strange sickness.

- Evil marks make you to struggle in all areas of life.

- Evil marks make you spiritually weak and dull.

- When evil mark is in your life, you begin to hear strange voices.

- Opportunity becomes difficult to come by in life, career and even in destiny.

- Evil mark enforces generational evil pattern. For example, if women in your family struggle in marriage, it's more than likely that an evil pattern is in place. If warfare prayer is not rendered, the situation will continue.

- Evil marks cause false accusation and unnecessary persecution.

- Evil marks could cause marital turbulence, divorce and separation.

- Evil marks open you up to satanic attacks.

- Evil marks could cause anti-marital problems.

- Evil marks make you a wander like a vagabond.
- Evil marks enforce bondage and slavery spirit.
- Evil marks make you experience hardship and poverty.
- How Do People Obtain Evil Mark?
- You can obtain evil mark through inheritance, transferred from generation to generation.
- Incisions are marks placed on your body either traditionally or self imposed.
- Carelessness by putting marks on your body like tattoo. "Ye shall not make any cuttings in your flesh for the dead, nor print any marks upon you: I am the LORD" (Leviticus 19:28).
- Redesigning your image: tattoos, sex change, skin bleaching, putting on hair from an evil altar.

HOW TO REMOVE EVIL MARK

1. Repent and turn away from sin and wickedness.

2. Surrender totally to Jesus Christ because you need His name, power and blood to be delivered.

3. Acknowledge that the mark is present even though it might be invisible to your natural eyes.

4. Plead and apply the blood of Jesus to cancel all evil marks.

5. Pray aggressively against this demonic weapon.

AGGRESSIVE PRAYERS AGAINST EVIL MARKS

1. Marks of darkness on my forehead, be cancelled by the blood of Jesus in Jesus' mighty name.

2. Blood of Jesus, wash away every evil mark attracting problems into my life in Jesus' name.

3. Inherited evil marks operating against my destiny be consumed by fire in Jesus' name.

4. Evil mark of demotion operating in my life, be destroyed by fire in Jesus' name.

5. Henceforth, let no man trouble me for I bear in my body the marks of our Lord Jesus (repeat seven times).

6. Mark of witchcraft tormenting my destiny, come out now and die by fire in Jesus' name.

7. Evil mark in my bloodline keeping me in perpetual bondage, your time is up, be roasted by fire in Jesus' name.

8. Divine mark of God come upon me now for divine protection and preservation in Jesus' name.

9. Every mark of poverty, struggle and delay be erased by the blood of Jesus in Jesus' name.

10. Powers chasing away my helpers, die in Jesus' name.

11. Wicked mark of my father's house upon my life, I am not your candidate, be wiped away by the blood of Jesus.

12. Strange voices speaking death and destruction into my destiny, be destroyed in the mighty name of Jesus.

Destroying Satanic Weapons

13. Blood of Jesus, sanitize my life in the mighty name of Jesus.

14. Ancestral marks troubling my life, be destroyed in the name of Jesus.

15. O God arise in your power and catapult me to another level in Jesus mighty name.

ABOUT THE AUTHOR

Prophet Isaiah Olujinmi was called into full-time ministry while preparing to enrol in a graduate program upon the completion of his bachelor's degree in politics and Criminology from Middlesex University, London, U.K. With the prophetic, deliverance and apostolic calling upon his life, Prophet Isaiah has ministered in many meetings around the world with the demonstration of God's power. He has planted churches in the USA, UK, and Canada. By the power of God, he is passionate about training soldiers of prayer that will travail in prayer and destroy the powers of darkness in order to reign as destined by God. With a profound heart for people, God has entrusted him with the prophetic gift to reveal His heart to His children, thereby edifying and fortifying the body of Christ.

Prophet Isaiah is the founder of Prayer Tabernacle International Ministries with the assignment to go from city to city, nation to nation and churches declaring the prophetic and demonstrating deliverance with the authority of God by FIRE. Prophet Isaiah has the passion to fulfill the call placed upon his life and to complete the race set before him by the power of God.

Fondly known by his humor yet delivering the message of God with power, many have been touched by God using him as a vessel. Prophet Isaiah is married to his childhood friend "Tosin" and they are blessed with three beautiful children: Isaac, Izabelle, and Israel. Together as a family, they are committed to fulfilling the plan and the purpose of God here on earth.

Isaiah Olujinmi

NOTE

NOTE

NOTE

NOTE

Isaiah Olujinmi

NOTE

NOTE

Isaiah Olujinmi

NOTE

www.ingramcontent.com/pod-product-compliance
Lightning Source LLC
Chambersburg PA
CBHW070649050426
42451CB00008B/327